Hidden Worlds

BEYOND THE BARS: EXPLORING THE SECRETS OF A Police Station

by Tammy Enz

Reading Consultant:
Barbara J. Fox
Reading Specialist
North Carolina State University

Content Consultant:
Mark G. Robbins, PhD
Assistant Professor of Law Enforcement
Minnesota State University, Mankato

CAPSTONE PRESS
a capstone imprint

Blazers is published by Capstone Press,
151 Good Counsel Drive, P.O. Box 669, Mankato, Minnesota 56002.
www.capstonepress.com

092009
005619WZS10

 Books published by Capstone Press are manufactured with paper
containing at least 10 percent post-consumer waste.

Library of Congress Cataloging-in-Publication Data
Enz, Tammy.
    Beyond the bars : exploring the secrets of a police station/by Tammy Enz.
    p. cm. — (Blazers: Hidden worlds)
    Summary: "Describes the behind-the-scenes places of a police station" — Provided
by publisher.
    Includes bibliographical references and index.
    ISBN 978-1-4296-3377-2 (library binding)
    1. Police — Juvenile literature. 2. Police stations — Juvenile literature. I. Title. II. Series.
HV7922.E69 2010
363.2 — dc22   2008054993

Editorial Credits
Jennifer Besel, editor; Bobbie Nuytten and Veronica Bianchini, designers;
    Eric Gohl, media researcher; Laura Manthe, production specialist

Photo Credits All images by Capstone Studio/Karon Dubke except:
Shutterstock/Andreas Bjerkeholt, throughout (concrete texture); Lagui, throughout (paper
with tape); Pokaz, throughout (grunge); Robyn Mackenzie, throughout (torn paper)

Table of Contents

CHAPTER 1

BEHIND LOCKED DOORS

Clang! A metal door slams shut behind the **suspect**. But this isn't the only locked door at a police station.

suspect — someone thought to be responsible for a crime

A police station is full of locked doors. Behind the doors are places seen only by criminals and cops. Now you get to see what's behind those closed doors.

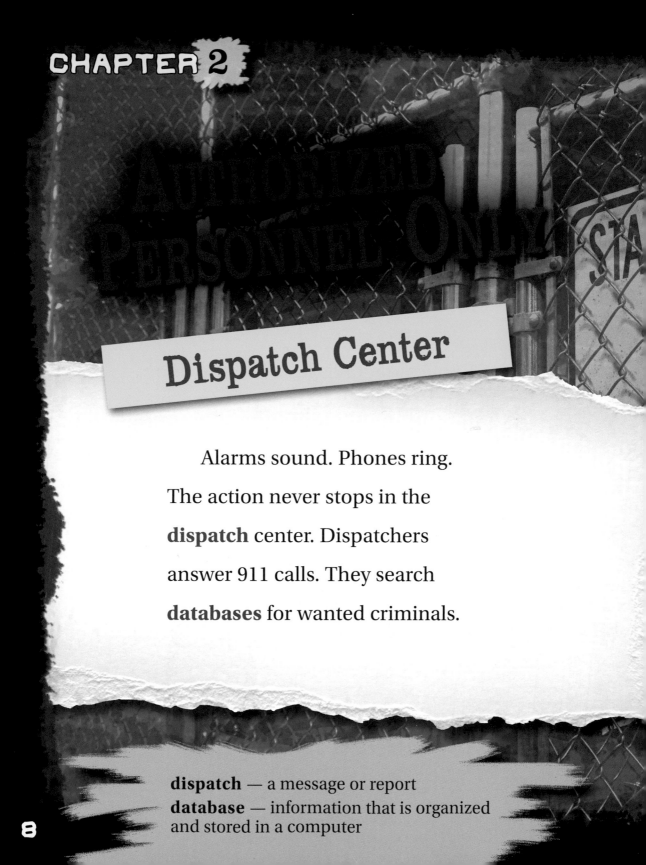

CHAPTER 2

Dispatch Center

Alarms sound. Phones ring. The action never stops in the **dispatch** center. Dispatchers answer 911 calls. They search **databases** for wanted criminals.

dispatch — a message or report
database — information that is organized and stored in a computer

INSIDE INFO

Dispatch centers in large cities answer millions of 911 calls every year.

Dispatchers control who comes in or leaves the police station. Officers in the dispatch center watch the doors on **monitors**.

monitor — a TV screen that is used to show what is being recorded

INSIDE INFO

Originally sally ports were built in castles.
Sally ports allowed fighters to get out but
kept enemies from getting in.

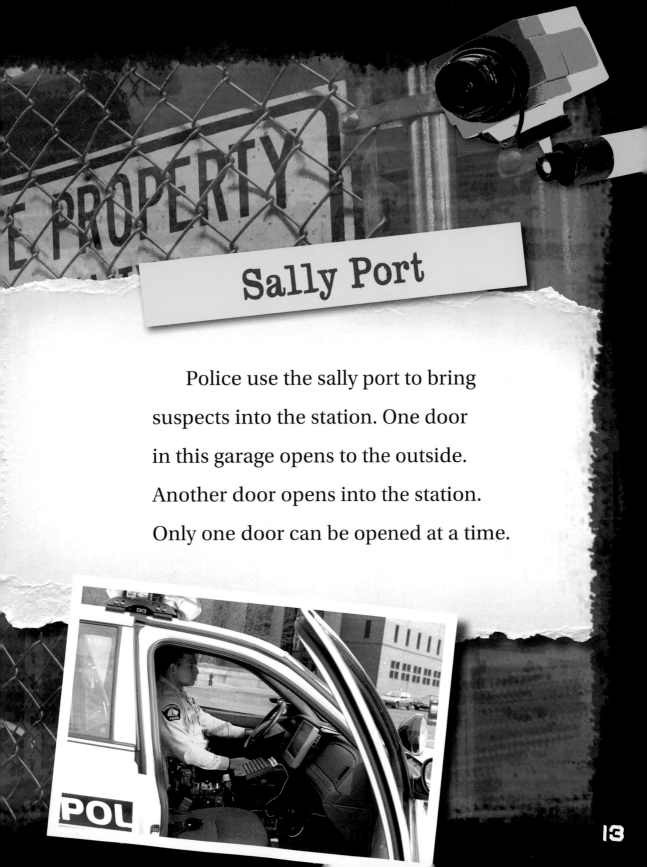

Sally Port

Police use the sally port to bring suspects into the station. One door in this garage opens to the outside. Another door opens into the station. Only one door can be opened at a time.

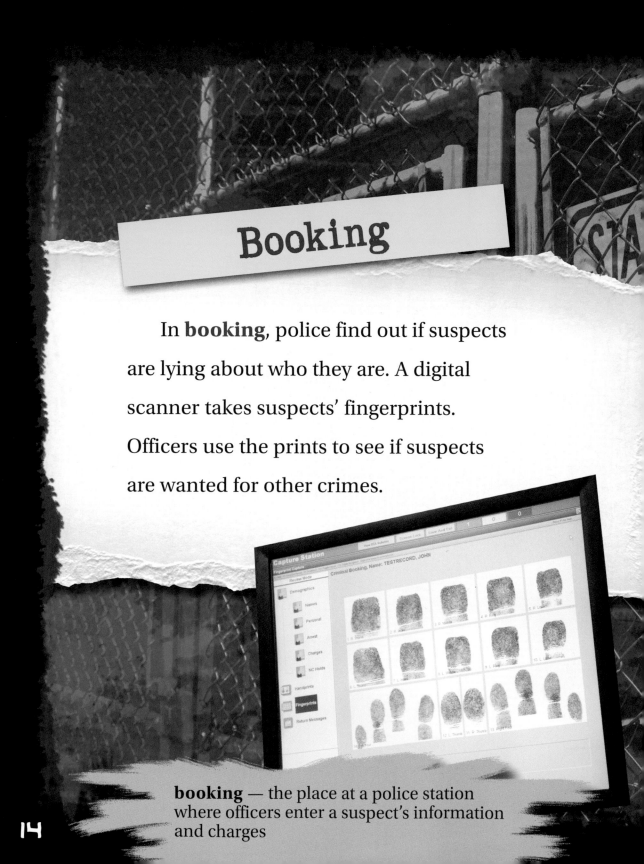

Booking

In **booking**, police find out if suspects are lying about who they are. A digital scanner takes suspects' fingerprints. Officers use the prints to see if suspects are wanted for other crimes.

booking — the place at a police station where officers enter a suspect's information and charges

Inside Info

Each day, the FBI receives about 50,000 fingerprints to add to its computer system.

Holding Cell

Suspects are locked in holding cells to wait for trial. Inside the cell, they can't even have their socks and shoes. A camera watches their every move.

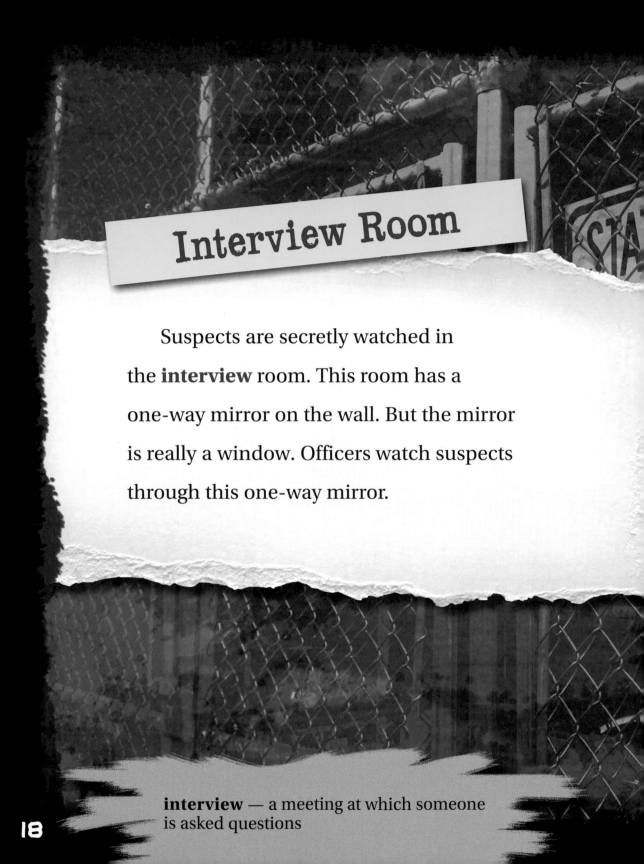

Interview Room

Suspects are secretly watched in the **interview** room. This room has a one-way mirror on the wall. But the mirror is really a window. Officers watch suspects through this one-way mirror.

interview — a meeting at which someone is asked questions

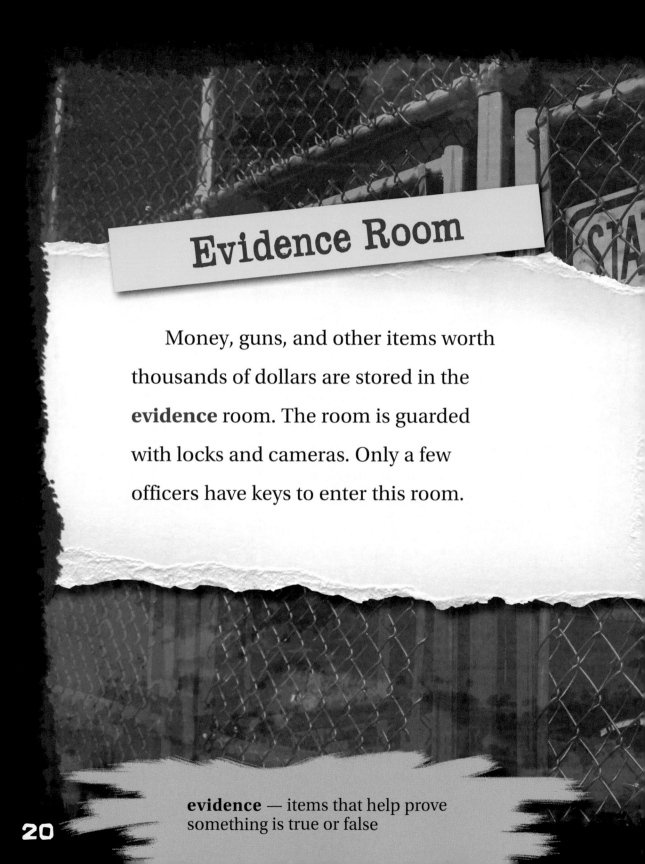

Evidence Room

Money, guns, and other items worth thousands of dollars are stored in the **evidence** room. The room is guarded with locks and cameras. Only a few officers have keys to enter this room.

evidence — items that help prove something is true or false

INSIDE INFO

Money and jewelry are stored in a safe
inside the evidence room.

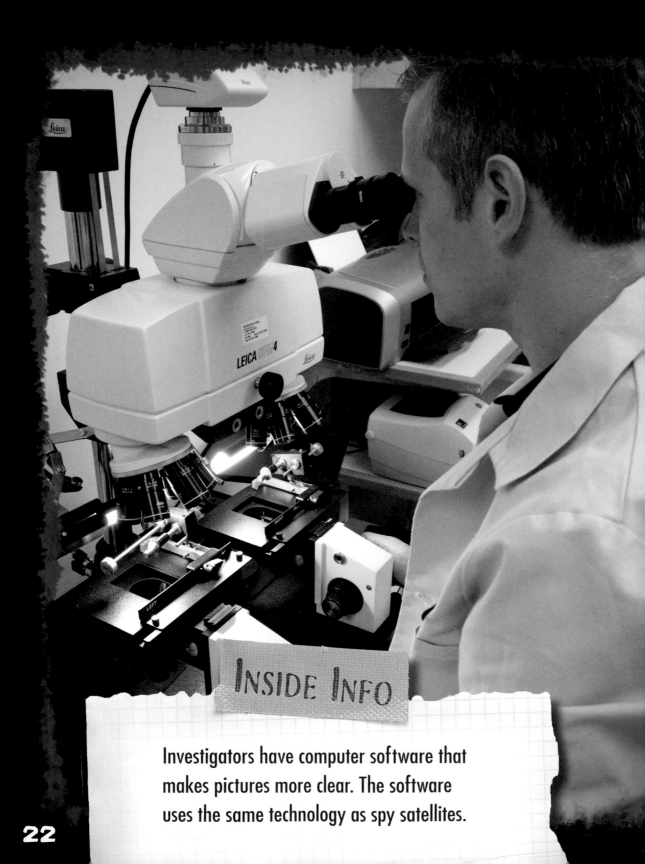

INSIDE INFO

Investigators have computer software that
makes pictures more clear. The software
uses the same technology as spy satellites.

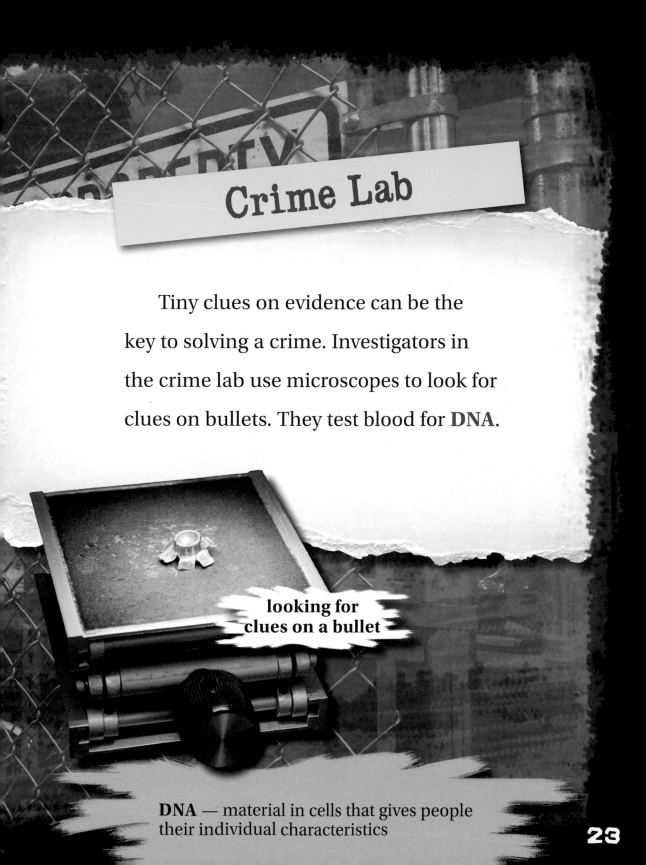

Crime Lab

Tiny clues on evidence can be the key to solving a crime. Investigators in the crime lab use microscopes to look for clues on bullets. They test blood for **DNA**.

looking for clues on a bullet

DNA — material in cells that gives people their individual characteristics

A speck of blood or a hidden fingerprint can help solve a case. In the crime lab, detectives use ALS lights to find these hidden clues.

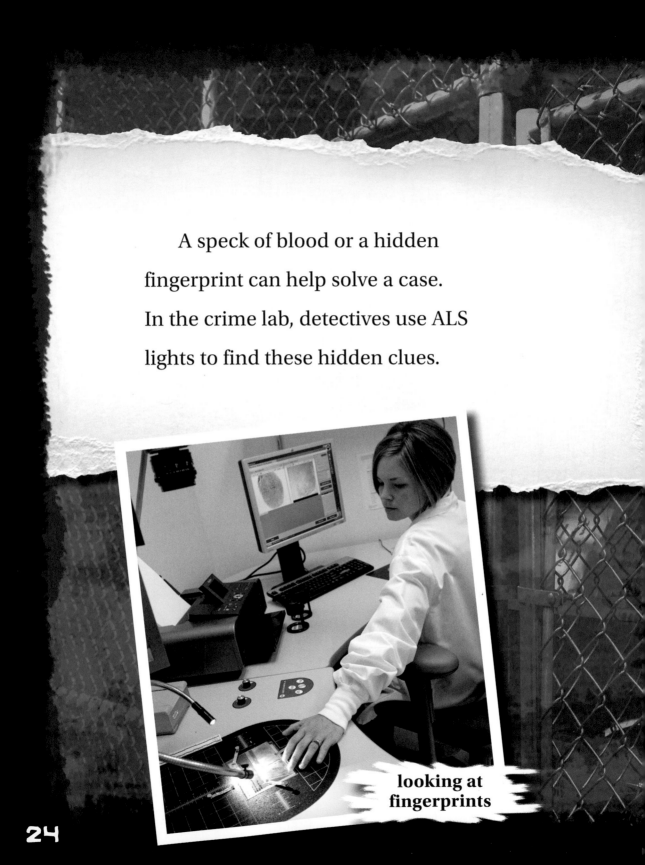

looking at fingerprints

INSIDE INFO

ALS stands for Alternate Light Source. This
tool shines colored light on pieces of evidence.
The light makes hidden clues show up.

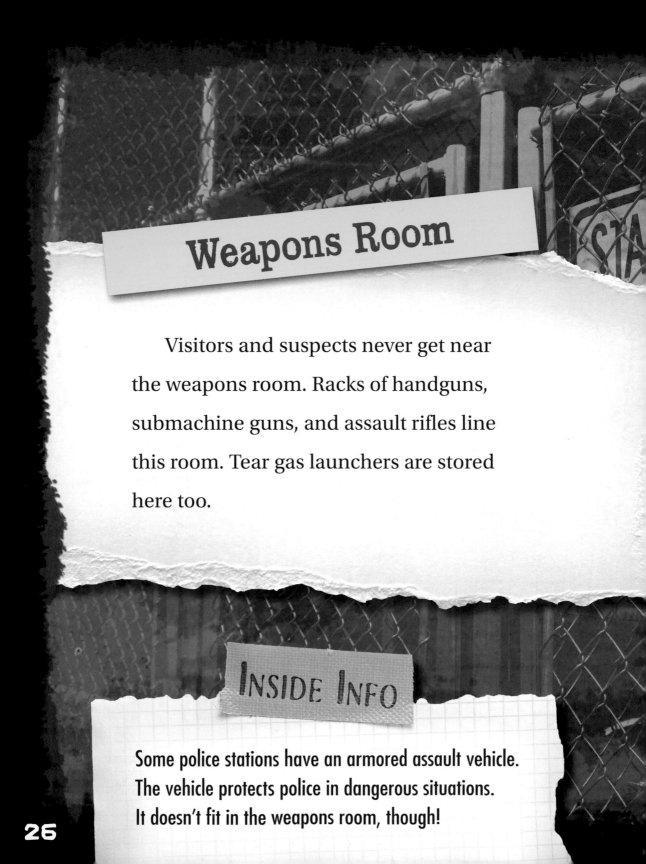

Weapons Room

Visitors and suspects never get near the weapons room. Racks of handguns, submachine guns, and assault rifles line this room. Tear gas launchers are stored here too.

INSIDE INFO

Some police stations have an armored assault vehicle. The vehicle protects police in dangerous situations. It doesn't fit in the weapons room, though!

armored
assault vehicle

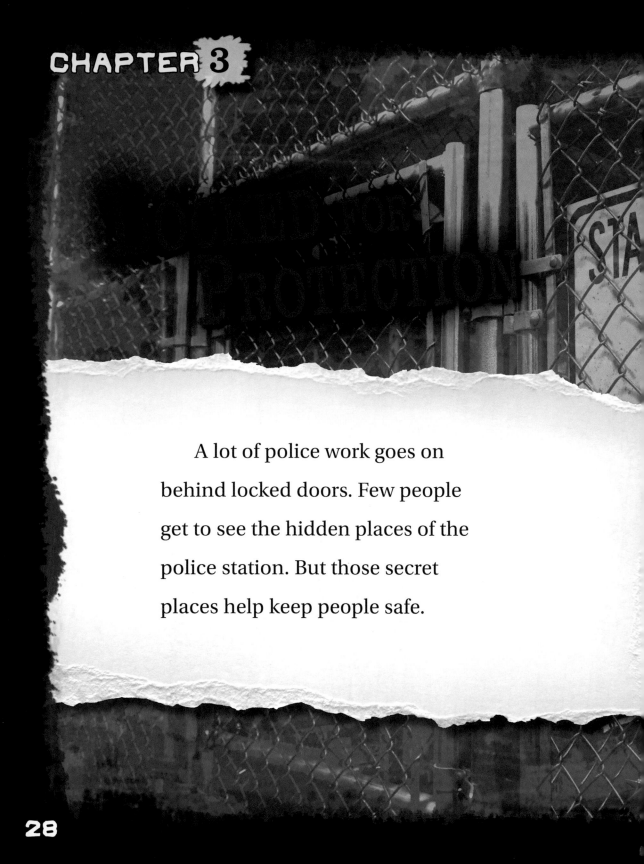

CHAPTER 3

LOCKED FOR PROTECTION

A lot of police work goes on behind locked doors. Few people get to see the hidden places of the police station. But those secret places help keep people safe.

Glossary

booking (BUK-ing) — the place at a police station where officers enter a suspect's information and charges

database (DAY-tuh-bayss) — information that is organized and stored in a computer

dispatch (diss-PACH) — a message or report

DNA (dee-en-AY) — material in cells that gives people their individual characteristics

evidence (EV-uh-duhnss) — information, items, and facts that help prove something is true or false

interview (IN-tur-vyoo) — a meeting at which someone is asked questions

monitor (MON-uh-tur) — a TV screen that is used to show what is being recorded

suspect (SUHSS-pekt) — someone thought to be responsible for a crime

READ MORE

Armentrout, David, and Patricia Armentrout. *The Police Station.* Our Community. Vero Beach, Fla.: Rourke, 2009.

Kenney, Karen Latchana. *Police Officers at Work.* Meet Your Community Workers. Edina, Minn.: Magic Wagon, 2010.

Miller, Connie Colwell. *Crime Scene Investigators: Uncovering the Truth.* Line of Duty. Mankato, Minn.: Capstone Press, 2008.

INTERNET SITES

FactHound offers a safe, fun way to find Internet sites related to this book. All of the sites on FactHound have been researched by our staff.

Here's all you do:

Visit *www.facthound.com*

FactHound will fetch the best sites for you!

INDEX